From Inside My Brain!

A poetic look at the world

By

Alan Claxton

ISBN-13 978-1492999898

Contents

3. Introduction
4. Horse V. Bicycle
6. The Noble Game
8. The Pantomime
10. The Tenner
12. Infinite Monk Theory
14. Nostradamus
16. How War Started
18. The Human Race
20. Weather Predictions
22. Nasal Infection
24. One More Beer
26. The Prospector
28. The Arrival
30. New Arrival
32. The New Rival
34. The Rivals
36. Birthdays
38. The Departure
40. Late Arrival
42. Valentine's Day
45. A Bunch of Flowers
48. Re-Patron-Is-Ed
49. The End

Introduction

Welcome one and all
To this poetry book of mine
It really has been fun to write
As I've thought about every line

The idea behind the poems
Is to welcome you to my world
Of looking at things quite differently
And let the humour within unfurl

I showed them to my closest friends
They said they're really good
Especially that type of humour
Which they totally understood

All examples have been tested
By some friends down at my local
The proof is in their laughter
And approval that's been vocal

Others I play a recording
In my taxi as they ride
So if it's ok for the local folk
Then let's try them country wide

Horse V. Bicycle

I was galloping at speed upon my horse
Across a local field
Rapidly approaching a five bar gate
I required the horse to yield

The horse was having none of it
Didn't do as he was told
Took off over the five bar gate
Which I thought was very bold

On landing he veered off to the right
And headed for a bike
Coming in the other direction
Which the cyclist didn't like

And so it was the horse and me
Against the bike and him
Since it was a narrow lane
The passing would be slim

The closing speed was so rapid
That soon we would find out which
Of these transport combinations
Would end up in the ditch

Now I could see it was the vicar
Cycling his way down to the church
And I'm sure I saw him praying
As the horse, he gave a lurch

At heart my horse is a jolly good soul
And didn't want to sin
Leaped clean over the vicar's head
The clearance was oh, so thin

We landed just behind him
And galloped off with relief
I felt a miracle had happened
An Act of God is my belief

But don't let the horse hear my thoughts
As he may well get the hump
'Twas he the horse that saved the day
'Cos he was the only one who could jump!

The Noble Game

Many years after the ball was invented
Throwing it by hand was becoming a yawn
It was more fun with feet, a ball to be kicked
And so the term 'Football' was born

It was considered good exercise in prisons
Where men would kick the ball at the gate
It would be saved by the gaol keeper
Which became 'goal' due to a spelling mistake

So the gate became a goal, represented by poles
With a net and a crossbar to boot
And the aim of the game was to tackle your mate
Which would give you a clear spot to shoot

But this became dull, just one set of poles
A situation they would have to amend
So after some talk of what would benefit the sport
They decided to have a goal at both ends

So now we had two sides of eleven men
Who would kick the ball from end to end
So when one side, the goal were attacking
The other side would try to defend

Then one day at a school up in Rugby
A lad picked the ball up and just ran
It saved all that fancy kicking around
Getting the ball over the goal line was his plan

He touched the ball down inside the goal mouth
Said the ref with annoyance, "Nice try!"
The lad shouted back, "What do I get for that?"
The ref with his fist clenched said, "I'll give you five!"

A bystander who was enjoying the action
Said "Five for a try, how about a goal?"
The referee turned round with a visual response
That's how we got two, so I'm told

So that's how the game of rugby began
It developed over many a year
It's made passing the ball by hand much more fun
And combined it with drinking good beer!

The Pantomime

Once upon a time, a man up in Blackpool
Had a horse outfit that fitted two men
With a friend, he performed on the stage
Mimed galloping around and panting at the end

The panting mime was a hit with the punters
Who would cheer and stand clapping for more
So the idea was born, for a panting mime horse
Which left the audience in a great state of awe

Increasing the fun for the people
He introduced a man dressed as a dame
To add a twist, a prince that was played by a girl
Create an entertaining show was his aim

Some tunes for the show were then written
Which have all become an integral part
By creating the mood in the theatre
Using them correctly is really an art

Then he added a cold hearted villain
So that the audience could all jeer and boo!
And a hero who would enter the action
So the crowd could shout out, "Behind you!"

As the hero looks to see who's behind him
Nobody is there to be seen
But as soon as our hero turns back to the crowd
The villain is back on the scene!

This part is for audience participation
Where the crowd can scream with delight
As they interact with the players
All part of this memorable night

Now the hero bamboozles the villain
Which to him is a poke in the eye
And gives a chance for the principal boy
To give herself a slap on the thigh

To finish with a feel good factor
It ends with a sing-a-long song
Then the players will take their ovation
With this formula, they couldn't go wrong

Now the ideas had all come together
To tell fairy-tale stories of old
Which would fit around all of the characters
And for theatres, many tickets would be sold

The tradition became to stage them at Christmas
Tell tales like Aladdin, Cinderella and Snow White
And have audiences in raptures of laughter
So everyone had a jolly good night

So now it's become pantomime season
Where the whole family can be entertained
Parents and children enjoy the show as one
Because a swearing ban has been retained

Now this story I tell you's a true one
"Oh not it isn't!" I hear you all wail
"Oh yes it is!" I give as my answer
This could go on, because it's worth telling the tale!

The Tenner

I work as a barman at the local pub
I've been working there for ages
Always looking forward to Friday
It's the day I'm handed my wages

In my wage packet, there is a tenner
On it is written a name
I wonder if this note is special
To spend it would be such a shame

The next day, before I go to work
My son says he's off to the fair
I reach in my pocket, it's the tenner
So I give him it, to spend when he's there

That night in the pub where I'm working
The fair folk come in from their day
One orders a large round of drinks
Some notes the man hands me to pay

While taking the money from him
There's a note I recognise straight away
It's the tenner with the name written on it
That I gave my son earlier that day

So I put the tenner in the till
Thinking, this is totally outrageous
I've just witnessed the cycle of money
Then come Friday, it's back in my wages

Next day, I give some money to my wife
Who says she's off for a shop
She's home just before I head to work
With pride, she shows me her new top

That evening I serve a nice young lady
Whose top is the same bought by my wife
Gives me a note, to pay for her drink
It's the tenner, it's true, on my life!

Again I put the tenner in the till
Thinking, can't wait until Friday is here
Sure enough, when I open my wages
You guessed it, the tenner reappears

My daughter says she's going to the coast
Off to the seaside with her best friend
From my pocket, I get out the tenner
Give to my daughter, for her to spend

Surely I will not see it again
The tenner will be spent far away
No one from that far comes to my pub
To buy a drink and with it to pay

On my day off, I'm in town with my wife
With a twenty, I buy some ice cream
I'm handed a tenner back with my change
As I look, I nearly let out a scream

Three guesses, yes it's the tenner
Which upon it is written a name
Never again will I try and spend it
Because it's hung on my wall in a frame!

Infinite Monk Theory

Some students at an end of term party
Wondered if 'the infinite monkey theory' was viable
Thought that Shakespeare was a little bit tricky
So instead they would tackle the Bible

They hunted around for typewriters
In the house they could only find one
So volunteered a lad to dress up as a monk
Which seemed apt and slightly more fun

They got the lad pretty well wasted
A willing sacrifice he would make for his art
And he typed the first chapter as, 'Genius'
Which to them was an encouraging start

The next little gem they discovered
Within a small amount of time they'd invested
'God created the university in six days
On the seventh God was arrested'

He typed away with even more vigour
The next bit was spotted with ease
The first people God had created
Went by the names, 'Edam and Cheese'

The typing was getting more rapid
At this speed he couldn't make a mistake
But, 'The forgotten flute in the guardroom
Was painted out to Cheese by a Sheik'

The last thing that was typed by the lad
Before he drunkenly slid under the table
Was, 'Edam and Cheese had two guys
They were named, Can and Unable'

Despite the hilarity that followed
The experiment was considered a fail
Because the monk had thought much too clearly
Evidently he hadn't drunk enough ale!

Nostradamus

Michel de Nostradame was an alchemist
And very good at his trade
So putting his great knowledge to work
A time machine he made

His desire was to visit Jesus' time
So configured his computer
But due to a miscalculation
He ended up in the future

He found himself in 2000 AD
Realising he had made a mistake
Conjured up a brand new plan
Which was a better path to take

He managed to find some history books
Which he sat and started to read
And jotted down many a note
Which would ensure his plan succeed

He closely studied from around 1550
Wrote down events, dates and facts
So on his return to his own time
Could write yearly almanacs

Now this, it gave him great credence
And success which he could savour
So put him with his prophecies
Into royal favour

Historical facts from his time
He must write them in disguise
So wrote loads of coded quatrains
To fool the church's spies

He thought it would be impressive
To predict the day the world would end
But looking through his many notes
Time after time he would have to amend

It could not be far from 2000
In his predictions, it felt very strong
Because the direction the world was heading
And types of weapons, it wouldn't be long

He even predicted the day he'd die
His genius we must not overlook
He knew it would all turn out that way
Because he read it in a book!

How War Started

Way back in ancient history
Some men settled and started farming
Hunter-gatherers would try to poach their stock
And they found this most alarming

So defences were built to protect their land
Made of wood and bricks 'n' mortar
So anyone who tried to intrude therein
The defenders would try to slaughter

And so some little conflicts began
Small skirmishes, but soon to expand
With armies involving lots more men
Would fight, to gain more land

It grew into county versus county
Each side headed by one man
Whose ego had got the better of him
So he crowned himself king of his land

He press-ganged lots of loyal followers
All battle armed for him to lead
And paid them if they didn't die
A few farthings with which their families to feed

These pretenders grew a lot more greedy
With masses of land in their hoard
Still not satisfied with what they ruled
Got boats, with which to go fight abroad

Now leading these invading armies
Were trusted generals who directed the field
While the king stayed home safe in his castle
Sent more men out to get killed

Now it turned into country to country
The king would send words to inspire
Send men to die in glory for him
So he could rule an empire

As these men grew even more powerful
With new weapons, that were built by the score
It would only take two of these egotistical men
To cause a global war

So it started with spears and swords
Then with different types of guns
And now with tanks, ships and planes
We've missiles and nuclear bombs

Now we are close to world destruction
I've a statement you might find alarming
None of this would ever have happened
If we hadn't started farming!

The Human Race

We think that as human beings
We are the cleverest in the world
But by studying other creatures
This theory can not be upheld

As babies we're born right useless
Takes us a year before we can walk
Where animals stand up in an hour
And fully grown by the time we can talk

We're built in God's image they say
Who's fine 'cos he's floating around
And leaves us down here a-struggling
With gravity holding us down

We have developed to stand up erectus
On two feet we see lots to gain
But you never see a horse with a back-ache
Or a cow with a walking frame

The wild animals sleep out in the fields
Some even kip on all fours
Where we need a nice comfy mattress
With all sorts of bedding and definitely indoors

You see, creatures have fur, scales and feathers
With chimps most like the human race
They have warm hair all over their bodies
Where we only have hair round our face

Now learning is a valuable commodity
We spend years obtaining knowledge in schools
Getting certificates for the smallest achievement
Where creatures are born knowing the rules

Like, to navigate we need a map and a compass
With bearings and knowing place names
Where birds and beasts travel for thousands of miles
With inbuilt knowledge and a very good aim

Crocodiles are immune to everything
The truth is they never get ill
We humans pick up every disease
And treat them with injections and pills

In the wild the alpha male is fittest
Breeds with females for the species to succeed
Whereas humans breed with anyone they fancy
Causing the strength of humanity to recede

That's why we have so many illnesses
Passed on by each generation of man
So as animals get more resilient
The human race goes down the pan!

Weather Predictions

A unique trait of these isles of Great Britain
Are all kinds of people who keenly endeavour
By a multitude of different methods
Attempt to predict British weather

There's a saying about red sky by shepherds
Which provides hope or maybe a warning
So it's delight, if it's red before going to bed
Or misery, if it's red in the morning

Then there're the cows who lay down in the field
Which means that it's going to rain
And a promise that it's going to be sunny
When they all decide to stand up again

Now it's going to be cold and quite breezy
When to the wind, the leaves turn their back
Which is not much use in the winter
When the evidence from leaves we do lack

Little white clouds form like mackerel scales
Are found high in the blue summer sky
Apparently this phenomenon only happens
When there's a promise of rain that's close by

From the coast looking far out to the ocean
You see white horses on the crest of a wave
There'll be not many fishermen going to sea
Instead, they stay home where it's safe

The prediction of snow is quite tricky
Because it relies on so many things
But it's said, when the north wind doth blow
We should expect the snow to begin

The snow can remain for days or weeks
Become icy and dangerous we know
But it's said, to expect more snow to fall
Before the rest of it goes

Now seaweed as a myth is a strange one
It goes wet if it's going to rain
My guess, it's likely to remain that way
Till we get sun and it dries out again

There's not many sayings for sunshine
They're about snow, wind and rain instead
So if you want a day out by the seaside
My suggestion is don't plan ahead!

Nasal Infection

The other day, I visited a friend
Not a good thing on reflection
He sat there coughing and sneezing
Appears I left with a nasal infection

Now this virus, it is annoying
Experience shooting pains in my eye
With tear ducts working overtime
My eyes are never dry

Then there are the sinuses
Which get blocked up from time to time
I get stuffed up in the warm indoors
But in the cold outside, I'm fine

Trying to sleep, is what I'm dreading
Which side to lay, is hard to tell
But when I wake up in the morning
Both sides are breathing well

So I think, I'll be alright now
The virus, it must have cleared
But, not long after waking up
That the symptoms have reappeared

Then my face goes sort of tense
Facial muscles start to seize
I know relief is on its way
As my face explodes into a sneeze

To choose a type of lozenge
Is a decision that one can face
The menthol ones seem the best
But leave an awful taste

There's a natural plant called Olbas
Comes in oil form, you can try
Breathe it in, it clears your nose
But stings if you get it in your eye

These remedies, tackle the symptoms
The virus, they no way stop it
The only way the doctors say
Is to use antibiotics

So many medicines I've accumulated
Kept in a drawer in which I rummage
But I see the better solution would be
To change my head like Worzel Gummidge

After the first sign of the virus
Take nothing and try to be strong
Your immune system should do its job
And in nine days it should be gone!

I Hope!!!

One More Beer

So, it's off to the pub
A plan clear in my head
I'll just have a couple
And then home to bed

As the evening continues
I've had eight or nine
And the barman is there
He's about to call time

Well, the bar steward refuses
To serve me one more
My glass is now empty
And I'm shown to the door

It's a long stagger home
But I'm feeling good now
'Cos it's straight up to bed
And this is my vow

But, when I get home
In the fridge I do see
A small row of cans
And they're winking at me

There's one in my hand
The ring is then pulled
This one goes down
It is nice and cold

Resisting another
Now this I will try
My will power diminished
I drink the fridge dry

With all alcohol gone
I crash in a heap
Don't care where I am
I just fall asleep

Wake up in the morning
My head is in pain
I've made the decision
Well, never again!

But as I feel better
As I go through the day
I think to myself
Well, I'll get some in case

So the afternoon arrives
And it's off to the store
To restock the fridge
Well, I'll just get the four

So, cometh the eve
What's to be done
Well I'll go to the pub
But I'll just have the one!

The Prospector

I am a prospector
Digging for gold
To find me some nuggets
Which when they are sold

Will make me a million
Well that is my aim
Trying my hardest
To win in this game

This dreaming of gold
Takes me to the brink
It drives me insane
And often to drink

I must make my fortune
Well that's my desire
But up to now nothing
The situation is dire

It's a dangerous business
That I face every day
I don't fear anybody
Who stands in my way

I play by the rules
But some don't abide
So, while I am working
I've got a gun by my side

I'm living the life
That could serve me well
So, who cares if I end up
Going to hell

It's better than lying
In a gutter somewhere
With another man's whisky
I'm begging to share

It's becoming a rich man
That matters so much
Because money means power
But that's not enough

To become the President
Where great status is held
Would be my chance
Of ruling the world

So, here I am standing
With a pick in my hand
All I have dug out
Is rock, dirt and sand

Digging so frantically
Out in the cold
Searching in vain
For my first piece of gold!

The Arrival

On a journey from where I do not know
In a craft I can't control
No windows to the outside world
No clue to what my role

A sleep I think I've had forever
No memories from the past
I find there's little room to move
How long is this to last?

But the engine seems it's beating fine
It's warm within my cell
Just murmurs from the outside world
And all is going well

Then suddenly there's a panic
My capsule's started leaking
I push to try to make my escape
Outside I hear some shrieking

As I emerge from the escape hatch
The light, intense in my eyes
I'm cold and very frightened
All I want to do is cry

My lifeline's cut away from me
As I scream with all my might
I'm washed, weighed and wrapped in cloth
And helpless in my plight

I've arms and legs I can't control
The world around's a blur
But my heart is beating, my breathing's fine
I'm alive and that's for sure

Then I'm placed in to the arms
Of somebody I do not know
But the sound of an engine beating
Is familiar from a while ago

So I must be on the mother ship
My capsule is still inside
So now I can rest at ease
As into sleep I slide!

New Arrival

Now that I've arrived
I'll strive to take control
Become a ruthless dictator
Although I'm not very old

I'll work out your routine
It will be different every week
Just to ensure that you
Are deprived of restful sleep

Your first job is to feed me
The milk it goes straight through
And if there's any excess
I'll bring it up over you

Your next job is to change my nappy
An aromatic parcel I make so well
You deserve a medal of honour
For dealing with the smell

Then half way through the change
I'll have a strong desire
To release a jet of number one
That could extinguish any fire

I will keep you on your toes
And have you wondering why
You think you've made me happy
And then, I'll start to cry

You think I've settled in my cot
And have drifted into a dream
But as soon as I think you've settled
I'll let out a mighty scream!

And if you try to leave me
I'll cry out crocodile tears
I can keep this up for hours
Until mummy reappears

If I can't get my own way
The thing that I will do
Is quietly hold my breath
Till I start turning blue

Next I'll throw a tantrum
When you'll wish that you could hide
This time I will be turning red
To let the devil within, outside

You see, I refuse to be responsible
At least, until I'm older
So will leave this heavy burden
Resting on your shoulder

So by the time that I have finished
You'll have aged twenty years for sure
And that is only the first year
So prepare for many more!

The New Rival

Mummy and Daddy are having a party
With their friends, having so much fun
Leaving me feeling a little left out
Don't they realise today, I am one

They pack me off to my grandma's
Who I'm unable to control at all
Whilst my parents remain at home
Relaxing and having a ball

Fast-forward to a few months later
I think I'm making mummy quite ill
She's tired, pale and putting on weight
Controlling her is no longer a thrill

In an attempt to cheer her up
I go from crawling to trying to walk
When I fall, there's a few little swear words
Well at least I'm endeavouring to talk

Then another few months pass by
I seem to be staying at grandma's a lot
She keeps telling me, I'm having a baby
I may be naive, but I'm not losing the plot

Come the day, we visit mummy in hospital
And they show me this scrawny little kid
Mummy tells me he's coming home with us
At this point, I'm flipping my lid

I'm informed that this is my brother
Who I should love with all of my heart
But He grabs all mummy's attention
So here's where the war with my rival starts

I try my hardest to get him into trouble
To get sympathetic love coming my way
All my plans generally backfire on me
Because he has the power at the end of the day

So I'm fast running out of ideas
All I end up doing is whining
I require a brand of amateur dramatics
Which a style, I'm currently refining

Now it's time to rethink my strategy
Where I've got to be smarter than him
So using my age and superior cunning
Let a different kind of battle begin

So now I've become very helpful
Also my dad's little chum
The benefit is getting me the best of both worlds
Leaving Junior crawling to mum

Years go by and I'm off to school
My new uniform makes me feel bolder
The great adventurer is on his way in the world
While Kiddo has to wait till he's older!

The Rivals

I enter my new classroom with apprehension
Considering if any friendships are viable
So until I get to know the other children
I see each of them as a possible rival

I find each child has a different characteristic
Assessed on my first days at school
Some of them are highly academic
Right down to the lad who's class fool

The kids pick on the fool as a target
He's teased and called terrible names
So anything that gets broke in the classroom
He's the lad who everyone blames

Another boy, he is the smallest
To a grasshopper, he's only knee high
It's a game played by the rest of the class
To make the little lad cry

There's a big lad who's considered class bully
He can push kids around with great ease
Sits on you until you cannot breathe
And never gives in to sobbing pleas

A group of girls who all stick together
Give the bully a run for his money
They're nasty and bitchy to the rest of the kids
And snigger as if it is funny

Then there're the swots, who gather in the corner
They have an integrated group of their own
So when the teacher asks the class a question
Theirs are the first hands to be shown

Some kids you find are best buddies
Next, you see them coming to blows
After a while they forgive each other
So their volatile relationship grows

There's a girl with a persona of glamour
Has lads eating from the palm of her hand
At her young age, she lights up boys hormones
In a way science can yet understand

Another girl the boys, she's always kissing
Makes many lads squirm with dismay
Only one lad would find this agreeable
He smells, so she stays away

The lad who only plays with the girls
With his poise and the way it is carried
He never joins in games of football
This boy is unlikely to get married

Making friends, I find real tricky
You have to rely very heavily on trust
I find most of the class unreliable
So most of my friendships turn into dust

So my strategy is now as follows
Be above average and just slightly keen
Hoping not to draw attention to myself
To be heard, but yet rarely seen!

Birthdays

Come this day for all of us
It happens every year
The receiving of many cards and gifts
Along with everyone's cheer

On this day you're made to feel special
With a gathering of family and friends
All there to celebrate your birthday
And so the great party begins

The presentation of the birthday cake
A telling number of candles on it, burn
As friends sing the happy birthday song
And wish you many happy returns

Your birthday when you're one year old
Appears, it's not for you at all
As you shouldn't know what day it is
It's your parents having a ball

Your party with school friends invited
At that young age is such a great thrill
Vast consumption of jelly and ice cream
With jumping makes most kids quite ill

From late teens and through your twenties
The celebration throughout the land
Is to party with lots of alcohol
And drink till you can't stand

Then you hit one of the landmarks
They generally end in a nought
The birthday you're forever dreading
Now here, not as bad as you thought

If you try to guess a person's age
It's hard to get a correct result
Some people you have complimented
Others you completely insult

To me birthdays are just a number
They're really not much fun
Just an indication of the times
I have travelled around the Sun

So it's the day I dread the most
The anniversary of my first breath
And not a single inkling
Of how close I am to death!

The Departure

So I've just completed my life
Full of hard work, fun and toil
I guess it was me who was next in line
To roll up my mortal coil

I stand here beside my old mate
The coat I have worn forever
Looking back upon the challenging life
My body and soul spent together

So the directors have taken my body
To what I assumed was the chapel of rest
But it ain't quite what I call dignified
More refrigerated warehouse at best

So the day's arrived, my own funeral
They've dressed me up nicely in my box
I wouldn't be seen dead wearing that suit
And definitely not together with grey socks

There's a random group of old crones
Visit local wakes of all who've expired
Dressed in black, round the coffin, all weeping
Gives new meaning to the term 'Town Criers'

To the Crematorium and the final service
Family and friends gather to say farewell
And hope to speak very highly of you
To prevent your soul going to hell

I remember the eulogy of Jack McJackson
Who was a rogue and a villain for sure
They said, he helped old aged pensioners
Yeah! Out of their money and making them poor

Another was Teddy O'Teddington
A dearly popular and charitable man
Who in his life cost charities dearly
And a smelly git that no-one could stand

I heard what they said at my funeral
He was a cheerful man and so full of wit
My interpretation of that statement
I was an annoying smirky-faced twit

Finally I heard a discussion
About the most important thing that I'd done
They came to a unanimous conclusion
I'd reduced the world population by one

In the end someone presses the button
The soles of my feet start getting hot
My whole body is turned into ashes
And I end up on the sideboard in a pot!

Late Arrival

I'm ascending the stairs up to Heaven
St Peter, dressed in white, is at the gate
With a copy of my Akashic records
His judgement will determine my fate

He is turning the pages at leisure
To me he is reading too slow
But then with a point of conviction
He indicates I should venture below

I look at him requiring direction
This time his actions are swift
Points out a door to the left
There's a sign up above it says 'Lift'

"Am I going to much higher places?"
"No!" he says, his chest starts to swell
"I can see no reason to let you in,
My friend you are going to Hell!"

I enter the lift, there's one direction
Nothing that indicates higher
Only one button is there to be pressed
And on it is a symbol of fire

Once pressed the lift starts descending
The journey took just a short while
When it stopped, the doors slid open
There stood Lucifer, with an extremely smug smile

I step out and greet him with a firm handshake
This I think must have caught him off guard
Because making the decision on whether to keep me
I could tell by his face, had made very hard

"So, why are you down here?" he asks
"I think that you've been misunderstood,
Seems the fires of hell aren't your calling,
Appears you've always tried to be good!"

So it's back in the lift I go
Back up to St Peter's domain
Who says, "You're still not coming in,
Instead you'll have to go live life again!"

So back down the stairs I descend
To the arrivals, with a question of 'maybe?'
Will I be animal or again human being?
Whichever, I'll start off as a baby!

Now, armed with a great deal of knowledge
I can tell the world, what they desire to know
But as soon as I've learned how to talk
I've forgotten the lot, what a blow!

Valentine's Day

It's Valentine's Day once again
So within that Twenty Four hours
You are required to buy your loved one
A card, chocolates and some flowers

The card should be Anonymous
You must not write from who
Which means your partner will guess
The card, It came from you!

But, if you have not sent one
And a card, it should arrive
Start questioning your relationship
And will it still survive?

Then if you have sent a card
And it's not the only one
Be sure she may be having
A little too much fun!

When Valentine's Day is finished
She's received no cards at all
It's likely that in the relationship
A veil of silence will now fall

Don't send a card too early
Or worse, a day too late
Or you'll find the dog's dinner
Is sitting on your plate

If she says, "not to bother!"
You think it is a trap
So, will you get away with it?
Or, will you get a slap?

For every loving couple
The restaurants, they will throw
A secluded candle-lit dinner
Where you both can go

With tables close together
Like sardines in a tin
Your shared romantic whispers
Will be swallowed in the din

Reserve your table early
For the night of pure romance
Try to book the night before
You hardly stand a chance

A three course dinner for fifty quid
To a couple seems quite nice
Any other night of the year
The meal would be half the price

A cheap old bottle of bubbly
Is offered with the meal
To celebrate your love
It's all part of the deal

Things are more expensive
To show your love to her
But makes a massive profit
For the budding entrepreneur

On going to the supermarket
Just after Christmas time
Shelves are stacked with lots of stuff
Relating to Valentine

There are hearts of different sizes
Chocolates by the score
And lots of cuddly animals
Need I tell you more!

I can't believe it starts that early
No sales I guess at first
Come February the Thirteenth
It goes in one short burst

There's all different types of men
Some you wouldn't like to fight
With card, roses and cuddly toys
Helps retain their conjugal right

Arriving home without a gift
Is a real man's fear
Because her who holds the power
He would be celibate for a year

To make a wrong decision
Or take an erroneous course
Could mean your precious marriage
Would end up in divorce!

So, let us do away with Valentine
Then we could all rejoice
Allowed to make our loving gestures
When we have made the choice!

A Bunch of Flowers

For months we've been busy at work
So I've been doing some extra long hours
And because I've seen so little of my wife
To show my love, I brought her some flowers

In return, I received a long hard stare
Cutting through me like a knife
The atmosphere that filled the room
I've never felt so heavy in my life

As the flowers came flying back at me
While she shouted, "How could you!"
Fighting off the shower of petals
I said, "What did I do?"

By now my head was spinning
And before I could recover
She had already left the house
And gone back to her mother

Before long I got a phone call
Getting verbal in the ear
I never knew her mother
Could be quite so severe

Before I had a chance to answer
The phone it just went dead
Which left me feeling very sick
And completely full of dread

Next, her father came a knocking
Says, "What you up to, son?"
"Doing lots of over-time!" I said
"That's all I have done!"

"Do you mean to tell me," said Pa
"You're not having an affair?"
"No!" I said most firmly
"It's only her love I share!"

Her father quickly left the house
Where I sat for what seemed like hours
Ruing the day that I had bought
My dear wife a bunch of flowers

Then like a sheepish figure
She crept into the room
"Please forgive me darling," she said
"I didn't mean to assume,

It was earlier this morning
When talking with my friend
She told me she was having
Affairs with other men

So, when I saw the flowers
I had the words fixed in my mind
And putting two and two to make up five
Sorry I was so unkind."

I said, "Oh let us forget it,
And now that you are here
Let's go down to the pub
And have a pint of beer!"

This episode happened years ago
We've looked back with lots of laughter
I've never bought her any more flowers
And we've lived happily ever after!

Re-Patron-Is-Ed

The Patron Saint of England
Was Saint Edmund years ago
Replaced by a Saint called George
Which struck as a bitter blow

What was St George famous for?
He was a dragon slayer from Greece
Whose cross was favoured in the crusades
So the white dragon of England was deceased

King Edmund he was martyred
St George a bit over-rated
For position of England's Patron Saint
St Edmund should be re-instated

With a local campaign underway
To get St Edmund back
I see only one tiny flaw
We'd have to change the Union Jack

Now St Edmund was an Anglo-Saxon King
There's a slightly more viable choice
He could be Patron Saint of East Anglia
Then we could all rejoice

Then an independent East Anglia
Could be our very next target
But to tidy up the border
We may have to lose Newmarket!

The End

Thank you for buying my book
I hope it was an enjoyable read
And if it made you laugh or smile
Then my purposeful plan did succeed

Many thanks till the next time